Operation Save Our Pastors

A Guide to Overcoming Pastoral Burnout

Dr. LeJoia I. VanHook, Ed.D

Copyright © 2018 by **LeJoia I. VanHook**

All rights reserved. No part of this publication may be reproduced, distributed, or transmitted in any form or by any means, without prior written permission.

Scripture quotations marked (KJV) are taken from the King James Bible. Accessed on Bible Gateway. www.BibleGateway.com. Scripture quotations marked (NIV) are taken from the Holy Bible, New International Version. Copyright © 1973, 1978, 1984, 2011 by Biblica, Inc.® Used by permission. All rights reserved worldwide.

Speak It To Book
www.speakittobook.com

Operation Save Our Pastors / LeJoia I. VanHook
ISBN-13: 978-1-945793-37-0
ISBN-10: 1-945793-37-6

First, I would like to dedicate my book to my very first pastor and first lady, Pastor Louis W. and Wanda Nance. You may have been small in stature, but your passion for the word of God was truly an inspiration and one to remember.

Second, I would like to dedicate my book to several people who have gone on with the Lord and left their footprints in my heart. All of these people were a part of my village, and I am truly grateful for them.

In loving memory of: Gerald VanHook, Darnell McKenzie, Kevin McKenzie, Verda Silas, Odessa Martin, Lawrence Taylor, Arthur Taylor, Mildred "Granny" Spain, James "Granddad" Spain, Ella Floyd, Rev. Leon Poe, Ethel Lewis, Connie McIntosh, Modena Smith, Veronica Jackson, Sterling McKenzie, and Kenneth Bowens, Jr.

I pray that I am making you proud! I will forever keep you in my heart!

Finally, I must dedicate this book to pastors who have succumbed to the stressors of pastoring and have taken or lost their lives because of it. You are remembered, and you are valued!

CONTENTS

Acknowledgments 3

The Calling 5

The Responsibilities of a Pastor 15

The Loneliest Profession 33

Challenges and Stressors Pastors Face Daily 45

Coping with Stress 59

What Every Pastor Needs to Know 75

What Every Congregation Needs to Know 89

You Are Not Alone 103

Notes 105

Pastor Responses 107

About the Author 123

About Speak It To Book 126

Acknowledgments

Greetings!

To God be the glory for *all* of the things He has done! The idea that I have written a book remains unimaginable and unbelievable, and I couldn't be more grateful. I'll never forget this journey.

I am so thankful, first of all, to God for calling me to complete this assignment. I know that this would not have been done if You were not by my side the *entire* time. You have allowed me to understand the pain, heartache, and disappointment that this group of people—pastors and their families—experiences on a daily basis. On the other side, You have equipped me with resilience and perseverance to endure the tough times. This book has allowed me to tap into emotions I have never encountered before. But one thing stands true above all: my faith and trust in You have graduated to a more advanced level in the course of writing this book.

To my parents: I am truly blessed to be able to call you Mommy and Daddy. You guys have shown your unwavering love and support in this season of my life. You have spoken life into my situations, prayed for me continuously, and shown so much consistency during this process. I am truly grateful for the advice and pep talks!

To my grandmothers, Irene and Betty: I love you both so much! I thank you for the influences you've had on my upbringing. I pray that you are proud of the direction I took in accepting my calling to this life. It is because of you and your prayers that I have committed to the work of the church. Thank you!

To my brothers and sisters (DeAnthony, Valerie, Michelle, and Damien): I love all of you so much! I appreciate your support, love, and laughter in this season. Thank you for everything you do for me.

To the remainder of my family (aunts, uncles, cousins, nieces, nephews, godparents, godbrothers, godsisters, and others): Thank you for your love and prayers. I truly appreciate your support, and I love you all!

To my church families, Original Philadelphia M.B. Church (Chicago, IL) and Tabernacle Baptist Church (Nashville, TN): You don't how much I appreciate you all! Thank you to the pastors, Demetrius Klyce and Darin Freeman, Sr., for connecting me with pastors for my dissertation. You both helped jumpstart this project so willingly that it brings my heart joy to know that I have your support in my corner. *Thank you for everything!*

To all of my friends: Thank you for checking on me and uplifting me in your individual ways. I love each and every one of you dearly!

INTRODUCTION

The Calling

Jesus went up on a mountainside and called to Him those He wanted, and they came to Him. He appointed twelve, designating them apostles, that they might be with Him and that He might send them out to preach and to have authority to drive out demons (Mark 3:13–15 NIV).

When Jesus called the first disciples, Mark tells us, their primary purpose was to be with Him. Only later, after a time of preparation and learning from Him, would they be sent out on their vital mission of preaching, healing, and deliverance.

As we know, these men ended up turning the known world upside down as Christianity took hold. But it all started with a calling.

Called to Serve

A strong leader can be defined as an individual who executes the leadership of others by influencing them to accomplish organizational goals, who sets an affirmative ethical tone, and who motivates others to achieve excellence. They can mitigate conflict and sustain change management by challenging the process, developing shared vision, and stimulating innovation and empowerment.[1][2]

Or, as John C. Maxwell put it, "A leader is one who knows the way, goes the way, and shows the way."[3] Pastors are known to possess those skills, and thus they fit the definition of a leader.

In Ephesians 4:11, Paul recognized people who have been given to the Church for special leadership roles: "And he gave some, apostles; and some, prophets; and some, evangelists; and some, pastors and teachers..." (KJV). When God calls and appoints someone to spread the gospel, there must be passion in their hearts for this lost and broken world—although there is often uncertainty regarding their own abilities. Being assigned so much power could be understandably overwhelming and even burdensome. On the other hand, to be equipped with such power is an indescribable feeling, one that requires much sacrifice and obedience.

Any leadership position brings with it a certain amount of stress. I have discovered that in a pastoral position the effects of stress can remain hidden to the casual observer and, left untreated, can culminate in a range of physical symptoms.

The pastor should recognize that they are regarded as an authoritative role model, mentor, guide, and often a spiritual counselor to their church members. As such, they can lose their identity as an individual, which in itself can be difficult.

Furthermore, unlike business leadership, for example, there is a supernatural element to this job. Pastors have the yearning to enrich their life journeys by making wise decisions through spiritual interactions with a "higher power" and guiding their followers to do the same. In other words, they desire to spread the gospel in their communities and bring people into a closer walk with God.

This supernatural element puts Church leaders in a league of their own, adding to the pressure of having to "get it right"—a sense of guilt for experiencing stress in such a godly calling. Surely it should be a constant joy and a privilege to lead God's people, right?

Pastors Lack Support

Yet, no one is exempt from experiencing struggles and difficulties, even pastors. Thankfully, we have the privilege of turning to our heavenly Father. We have instruction in the Bible, the guidance of the Holy Spirit, and the blessings of prayer.

Yet there are times when we feel the need of another human being, a wise and experienced advisor, to support us through a difficult time. At these moments, many of us turn to our pastor for prayer or advice.

I have experienced enough troubles in my life to recognize this trend. I have also been in the Church long enough to witness church members adding their names to the prayer list. Anytime I encountered turmoil, I, too, solicited the prayers and advice of my pastor. Later, when I got back on track, I often wondered about the pastor's own support system. Where does a pastor go when he or she is in desperate need of assistance to survive the daunting demands of such an influential position? To whom can a pastor turn without worrying about being rejected, viciously judged, or simply attacked? What are some healthy solutions for pastors to cope with these wearisome issues? Could church members do more to offer our support?

As a child, I never understood the true burdens of a pastoral position until my godfather showed me the ropes by taking me along with him while he fulfilled his duties. I began to see that life at the front of the church is not all it appears from sitting back in the pews on a Sunday morning.

As well as a preacher, the pastor is an administrator, a community activist, the spiritual leader of a congregation, and an evangelist, among other roles. The pastor christens the infants, baptizes the newly saved, counsels and marries the adults, and buries those who pass away. The pastor is also a servant-leader responsible for maintaining the spiritual edification of the congregation. Living up to all of those roles can be a formidable challenge filled with stress for any person.

The crazy part about most pastors I know is that they experience genuine fulfillment regardless of the high demands placed upon them. I am continuously baffled yet intrigued about this. No wonder, then, that I decided to research the area of stress management and pastoral leadership for my dissertation.

The Study

This book is based on the findings from the study I implemented for my dissertation, including interviews with an anonymous group of male African-American Baptist pastors who kindly shared both their struggles and their survival techniques. Leadership can be very lonely and dismantling, yet most times it seems that pastors struggle with appropriately facing their issues in a healthy manner for a number of different reasons.

While I was collecting data for my dissertation, the pastors I interviewed were transparent in sharing their experiences, for which I am eternally grateful. Their stories were fascinating, challenging, and heartbreaking to hear. Knowing what I know now, it's surprising to me that any pastor can survive, let alone thrive, in their ministry.

One pastor shared that he initially didn't take his calling seriously. He was still going out and doing what he wanted to do (from a worldly perspective). These actions led to infidelity in his marriage. It wasn't until after he committed adultery that he realized God was giving him another opportunity to minister to others. Thankfully, he was able to reconcile things with his wife, and now his marriage is stronger than ever. He shared that the ministry does present a great amount of stress and temptation, but what matters is how pastors respond to these challenges.

Another pastor shared that social media drove a wedge between him and his now ex-wife. He told me that he removed himself from social media and left his previous church because his church members would take pictures of him out for meetings and post them to social media, all while tagging his wife. His marriage broke down, and, not surprisingly, he found himself in a negative state of mind toward the church after enduring such insensitivity and turmoil.

Setting the Scene

The overall research question that I proposed had the following specifics involved: Is there a connection between emotional stress and Baptist pastoral leadership? My study explored not only the effects of emotional stress, but also effective strategies that may help reduce stress in the pastoral context.

As previously mentioned, very little research has been done relative to leadership and stress management in religious organizations. I wanted to fill this gap in the research base. In an effort to better understand the relationship between pastoral leadership and stress management, I used what is known as a qualitative research methodology. In other words, I interviewed a group of pastors to learn what pressures they are under and the effects of that pressure on their daily lives.

As well as looking into the everyday life of America's Church leaders, I wondered about the ways they are portrayed in the media. Why does the news media depict pastoral leaders and ministers as those who deprive others of their money and spiritual growth to their own advantage? How does a negative and sometimes false portrayal affect a leader's character, when it has been the populace who devised the image and placed them on a platform in the first place?

The reality of a pastor as an individual with shortcomings that all human beings possess, along with the false perception of society that pastors are somehow "faultless," places undue stress on them. Individuals in this situation often experience a mental heaviness when leading congregations in the right direction of spirituality. Daily stress, which increases over time, can ultimately cause pastors to reach a breaking point. At this stage, they might turn to drugs and alcohol, sexual immorality, or physical abuse, or even suffer from physical and psychological disorders.

The purpose of my study, and indeed this book, is to understand pastoral leadership and pastoral stress, and to identify common and effective strategies for managing that stress. I want to do that by describing pastoral stress and coping mechanisms from the point of view of the pastors who participated in the interviews.

My primary research questions were as follows:

Research Question 1: Is there a link between emotional stress and Baptist church pastors?

Research Question 2: How do Baptist church leaders manage negative stress?

Research Question 3: How can undue stress be managed effectively?

Meet the Pastors

Thirteen male, Baptist pastors agreed to be interviewed anonymously. For purposes of this book, I refer to them by pseudonyms: "Pastor Steven," "Pastor Dwight," "Pastor Paul," "Pastor Harris," "Pastor Smithson," "Pastor Trenton," "Pastor Wright," "Pastor Randall," "Pastor Lowe," "Pastor Summers," "Pastor Jake," "Pastor West," and "Pastor Blake."

The pastors lived in two places, Nashville and Chicago. They ranged in age from thirty-four to sixty-three years. Five were less than forty-years-old. All were currently married except for Pastor 10, who was divorced. They worked an average of 55.77 hours per week for the church (minimum ten hours, maximum 120 hours) and had been with their current church an average of 13.42 years (minimum 3.5 years, maximum twenty-four years).

Despite their anonymity, the pastors' different personalities come across in their comments, and I hope you will enjoy getting to know them.

At a time when more leaders than ever before are leaving the ministry through "burnout," it is vital that church congregations everywhere learn what they can do to support their pastors. I have two goals in writing this book: first, to help pastors and their congregations better understand the pressures they face, and second, to show what both sides can do to lighten the load.

This book is written out of obedience to God. If you are reading it, you didn't pick it up by chance. I truly believe that God is reconstructing His Church as we shed light on most, if not all, that pastors encounter daily. The struggle is real, but hardly anyone talks about it. Well, that ends here and now!

My aim is to reduce—and ultimately put an end to— the emotional and spiritual distress in which pastors often operate. I pray that this book reduces the degree of depression and the risk of suicide that exist with a role in pastoral leadership and that it helps the Church to reevaluate the expectations and demands that it places on her pastors.

And so I pray, too, that as you read this book, respond to the workbook questions, and undertake the action steps, you will keep these purposes held close to your heart. Choose to take part in Operation Save Our Pastors!

14 · LeJoia I. VanHook

CHAPTER ONE

The Responsibilities of a Pastor

In my research, I asked the pastors a series of questions about being a pastor. Their answers highlight their personalities, perspectives, and circumstances. As will become clear, each pastor is his own man. The pastors I interviewed spoke from their own experiences and offered a range of viewpoints.

What Qualities Should a Pastor Possess?

When I asked them what characteristics every pastor ought to possess, their answers covered a variety of good deeds and blessed intentions that can be summarized as: faith, the Holy Spirit, humility, integrity, willingness to listen, longsuffering, patience, character, and passion— with a healthy dose of lunacy mixed in!

Pastor Smithson had the most comedic answer, so this section about the qualities needed in a pastor starts with him. He listed two important characteristics, one quite humorous: "What I believe every pastor possesses? I've got an answer, but I'll give you the on-the-record answer and I'll give you the off-the-record answer. The on-the-record answer is every single pastor possesses passion. The off-the-record answer is every pastor possesses lunacy. Like being a lunatic! You have to be crazy to be a pastor!"

When prompted for his reasoning, Pastor Smithson offered this insight, "Because pastoring will always take you beyond the historical logistics that you're used to. You have to have the ability to go beyond what you've always known in order to service people that you've never encountered before. So, in order to go beyond what's sane and logistically possible, you have to be crazy...."

Pastor Smithson's comments mirrored a similar joking aspect in Pastor Trenton, who, when asked what advice he would give someone going into a pastoral position for the first time, replied, "Run!"

Pastor West also called for passion, adding, "If I don't have passion for it, you know, it'll never get done—or if it does, it'll take a long time."

Pastor Steven gave the answer of humility: "Because this will humble you if you're not already there, and if your ego's not ready for that, it'll crush you. It can."

Pastor Dwight answered "service" and then changed it to "humbleness," because "You need a humbleness—that's probably the word—in as much as we can be the head [person] in charge. We've still got to know that we came to serve the people. You hear me say it all the time. I never introduce myself as a pastor. I'm the servant. I serve the church."

For Pastor Randall, every pastor has "to have faith. You have to *believe God*, [not just] believe *in God*, because those are different things. To believe God is to believe what He says and do it. Believing in God, you know, we believe in the Easter Bunny...."

Pastor Paul argued for "commitment, dedication, faithfulness. All synonyms. You know, you have to have that passion to do it, to want to be there. The patience to wait. The commitment."

Like Pastor Paul, Pastor Wright called for faithfulness: "A pastor needs to be faithful." He followed this with a rhetorical question: "Who is going to follow a pastor who is not faithful to what he is teaching and to what he is preaching?" He continued:

And that faithfulness should be in your walk with God in terms of allowing the people to see your faithfulness to the different things that you have taking place at your church. It doesn't look good if, you know, the pastor—he's only coming in there to preach, teach, and get a check, and he's gone. He needs to be a part of it. If there's going to be witnessing on the streets, he should be there. If there's going to be a missionary meeting, he should be there. And he shouldn't just be present—he should be a part of it.

And then, too, they can see the faithfulness that he has toward not only the ministry, but also his faithfulness to his spouse if he's married. They should see him in operation with his wife. He should be faithful to his wife.

He should be faithful in every aspect of his life. It requires faithfulness. So that would be one of the core values: faithfulness.

Pastor Wright's comments on faithfulness expanded from the pastor's walk with God to include involvement with church members and activities, despite the potential pressures of doing so and warnings from some pastors to maintain a "mystique"—that is, a degree of separation to underline the pastor's authority. He also addressed the importance of faithfulness in a pastor's personal life, such as to his wife.

Like Pastor Paul, Pastor Trenton called for patience, because in the eyes of God, we are all children, and children need repetition:

> Patience. You know, early on in my ministry, I had not learned patience. I have all the patience in the world when it comes to children, when it comes to young people, because they're supposed to have to be told more than once.
>
> But it took a while for me to learn that even with us as adults that we're yet children in the eyesight of Christ. So, it takes a while sometimes for people to catch on to what they're really supposed to be doing. We have to have patience with them, you know, just as Christ has patience with us.

It would take both faithfulness and patience to exhibit the characteristic that Pastor Summers thought every pastoral leader ought to possess: long-suffering.

> I'm sorry. Paul said that we are prisoners for Christ, and in a way we are. Preaching can be one of the most warming fields in the world, and yet, at the same time, it can feel like a prison because there are places you can't go and things you can't do and people you can't be around. And it can feel like a prison.

And then you deal with people that are supposed to be saved and sanctified and they do everything but that. When you try to have a life, they tell you, "Oh, Reverend, you shouldn't do that!" When you go sit down somewhere, they say, "Reverend, you ought to go somewhere [else]."

So, long-suffering, because you know, you just, you never get comfortable, you never quite fit in a niche. It's always something. It's always something. So, long-suffering, that is a quality that every pastor needs.

Pastor Summers went on to speak of another characteristic he felt is needed—channeling the will of God through the Holy Spirit:

The other quality that I think every pastor needs is the Holy Ghost; that's actually in our Baptist church, you know. The very first paragraph of the Baptist church covenant talks about that we do these things with the aid of the Holy Spirit.

There's nothing we can do without the aid of the Holy Spirit, because if we went on our own personalities and whatever else, we would not be successful at all. Because we would pick and choose who to go visit, and pick and choose who to counsel. You've got to have all of those things. Because you ... you've got to have love, you've got to have this, you've got to have that. You can't have nothing unless you've got the Holy Ghost.

Pastor Harris called for integrity, because without it a church leader cannot get their pastoral work done. He provided evidence of this theme of personal growth in his insights. Just as he thought his job was to grow spirituality in the congregation, he strongly advocated for his own, and for other pastors', self-growth:

20 · LeJoia I. VanHook

> I think integrity is a very important characteristic of the pastor. Without integrity in a pastor, I don't think you can establish any trust among your congregation. I don't think that there would be any power in your preaching, in your studying.
>
> Integrity pretty much goes through the whole thread of pastoring. You have to have integrity in your sermon preparation. There are a lot of preachers, pastors that plagiarize their sermons. They get them off the Internet. There is no time spent in studying. The same thing relates to Bible studying.
>
> I think that the pastor should take time out of his schedule to adequately prepare for sermons, for Bible studies, to grow ministries, other projects that the church tends to be involved in. I think that should be done with the spirit of integrity. If there is no integrity in the pastor's overall ministry, it will reflect in the congregation.

Pastor Blake's thoughts were along the same lines as Pastor Harris's: "Integrity, integrity, yeah, yeah." He gave similar reasons to Pastor Harris's, "Well, because if the people don't trust you, you can't lead them. They've got to trust you. They've got to know that no matter what, you're going to do what is right. You're going to make the right decisions and do your best to be right, to do right."

Pastor Lowe called for a characteristic that differed from the others but is essential to pastoral work—the ability simply to hear people, "A lot of times we listen but we really don't hear them. And I think when people see that we're not only just listening to them but we're hearing them, then they come to appreciate us more and become more dependent. Well, not so much dependent, but become more appreciative, attentive, and even inviting of our claims."

Based on the pastors' responses, it is evident that there is a high standard placed on them for their character and lifestyle. In addition to the expectation for the quality of their character, they are also expected to make weighty decisions.

What Are a Pastor's Most Important Decisions?

Everyone knows that the pastor is responsible for making most of the decisions for the church, alongside the deacons and the trustees. So, what are the most important decisions a pastor faces? The pastors I interviewed provided a number of different viewpoints on the most important decisions they are charged to make.

Four pastors (Pastor Steven, Pastor Dwight, Pastor Smithson, and Pastor Summers) said that the decisions corresponded to all-purpose management of the church. Another four pastors (Pastor Trenton, Pastor Blake, Pastor Wright, and Pastor Harris) said the important decisions are a blend of administrative and spiritual needs. Pastor Jake focused on human resources. Pastor West gave the deepest spiritual response. Pastor Randall felt his own well-being was a key factor in order to stay balanced and, therefore, effective.

Pastor Lowe took issue with the interview question itself, arguing that "pastoring is not a decision-making [process]. Decisions are created on their own as situations arise." The way he saw it, decisions created their own momentum and resolution, and he was just the mediator. It turns out he had a specific and somber situation in mind:

> I guess I'm wrestling with—I don't have the authority to tell a family that it's time to remove their loved one from life support. I don't have that authority to say do it or don't do it. But I do have those moments when I have to share with the family that modern medicine has done all that it has to do and you've done all that you can do. There is nothing else to be gained in prolonging the inevitable. And so, if I had to make a decision, it would be when to tell that family. But that's not something I would do every day. That's an as-the-case-may-be situation.

Pastor Steven and Pastor Dwight both revealed that the most important decisions they are called upon to make correspond to all-purpose church management, with the unspoken risk that shepherding the flock could easily become lost in the shuffle.

Pastor Steven described the important decisions as, "Vision, strategic planning, staff hiring and redirecting, budget, budgeting priorities, sermon prep, what we call spiritual direction. You can't call it counseling unless you're certified to do counseling. These are pastoral decisions."

Pastor Dwight thought the most important decisions from his perspective are, "Directing funds where most needed, which sometimes prioritizes something that's neglected. Managing personnel. Innovation, of course, trying to do things differently and better. Trying to meet as many needs as possible within our capabilities."

Pastor Smithson needed some clarification, which underscores the complexity of running a church. He then addressed administrative needs, up-to-date information, and human resources as key areas for decision-making:

> [The most important decisions are] administrative: Who is the appropriate person to place in the appropriate role so that the mission and vision are accomplished effectively? The second most important decision is which information to use for study purposes, so that you provide the most accurate and up-to-date information to lead. Third most important decision is the human [factor]: Which human resources do you choose, what human resources do you allow to invest in you so that you are properly shaped for the ministry? That's probably the top three.

Pastor Summers also talked about administrative concerns, demonstrating how the constant demands on the pastor's attention act as a source of stress:

> I don't pastor a big church, and so I make all the decisions for the most part. I don't have all of those different boards and all of that stuff, so I pretty much make all the decisions. I have deacons and things that I consult, but the final decision is mine.

> Also the areas of contracts, finances, organizational structure, how to handle—I don't even know how to word this—how to handle the issue of the day. That's my biggest one. There's always something, so whatever the issue of that moment is.

Pastor Trenton felt that the most important decisions he makes are a blend of the administrative and the spiritual needs of the people. But he put more focus on the personal and spiritual needs of the congregation than on running the church:

> Well, I guess it starts out with me in seeing what the church may need spiritually and trying to bring about the plan to strengthen them and nurture them in their growth with Christ. But what happens is, along with that, we have the day-to-day operations of things. Naturally, you know, you're building the people in general.
>
> You know, you have to see to the welfare of the people in general. People have all types of problems and in having those problems, you know, we have to be able to discern them sometimes. Sometimes the people won't tell you right out. But then, as the pastor, as the leader, you need to know when something is wrong with the people.

Like Pastor Trenton, Pastor Blake was mainly focused on the spiritual needs of his flock but necessarily grounded in the business model. He also included the pragmatic needs of running the church.

> Well, of course, number one is basically the spiritual direction of the church, so you know [you are] making sure that, from a spiritual standpoint, the church is growing spiritually. So that includes, of course, Bible class lessons, sermon preparation—that kind of stuff. You know—anything that has to do with cultivating a going-to-church spirit. So that's a huge decision, number one.
>
> Making sure, number two, that leaders are in place to complement the different ministries that they're over.

So, basically, putting the right people in the right place—that's a big decision. As well as the financial goals, you know, making sure that the finances and everything is intact and all that good stuff.

For Pastor Wright, the most important decisions were also about the needs of the congregation, in this case conforming to gospel teaching and the need for discipline:

Well, inside of the church, especially in recent years, there have been a lot of different things that people want to bring into the church that don't necessarily coincide with the doctrine of the church or the accurate teachings of our particular local body. And so there are some things that sometimes you have to stop.

But then, too, sometimes it's out of the church, where you have people who have been a part of the church for a while that they—they're not very open to the new ideas or the new believers, the new people that come into the church or those that even grew up, maybe, in the church under them. They still view them as being children or young and they don't [know] anything. So, there are times when the pastor has to step in. And it's not so much that I issue discipline as much as maybe I may be stopping a few things that, you know—that I don't feel as though they're being encouraging.

Sometimes it is discipline. I have to sit someone down or even tell them that, you know, maybe they may be suspended from a position or something like that they may be holding in the church.

In Pastor Harris's opinion, the most important decisions were not about administrative management, "As a pastor I think that, as it relates to me, the most important decision that I have to make is making sure that the people are spiritually fit or that they are developing in their spiritual lives. And so that would consist of preaching and teaching and then trying to measure some type or level of growth in the lives of the congregation. The most important job is making sure that they're growing spiritually, that their faith is being strengthened."

Pastor Jake added that important decisions also involve delegating roles to other people, "You know, I think [student] vision is one. I think the other is building teams, determining who is going to be working on teams to execute projects. Think you have major decisions around those two areas, mostly. Student vision and then also deciding who's going to execute the vision based on their capacity, competence, etc."

For Pastor West, none of the above considerations entered into his equation. His view was one of deep spirituality: "Well, one is, whose voice will I heed, God or me?" Then he added two more: "What direction you take when it comes to the issues of social justice? And that was also our response to governmental action."

For Pastor Randall, the most important decisions were deeply personal, but one could argue that they ultimately contributed to his mental well-being and balance. Pastor Randall was the pastor who pointed out, poignantly, the risk of being a public success but a private failure. His most important decisions are:

What's going to matter in your life and how you're going to rate yourself a success. Yeah, I think that'll kind of be the seminal ones. What's going to matter to you? Is it going to be standing up in front of a lot of people? Is that success for you? I mean, you know, is money going to be success for you? Is building a strong church going to be success for you, or is being a solid Christian going to be a success for you?

Most of us choose the top options and might be successful in those regards, but, you know, you go home with them and your wife don't think anything of you. And your kids don't either.

That's a failure to me. That's a public success, but a private failure. The most important decision I've made is to try to be a good Christian and to be a responsible steward of everything that the Lord has placed in my life and in my care. That includes the ministry, but also my family. It means that I have to be pastor, but also a witness to the gospel in my personal life.

With so many decisions resting on the shoulders of pastors, it is no wonder they experience high stress levels. The following chapters will further explore these unique circumstances and stress factors the pastors face in their profession.

WORKBOOK

Chapter 1 Questions

Question: Why are integrity and faithfulness such important qualities for a pastor to possess? What are some other vital qualities? What are the qualities God ranks as most important in 1 Timothy 3?

Question: What are some of the hardest decisions pastors face? How are these different from decisions faced by lay people?

_____

_____

_____

_____

_____

_____

_____

_____

_____

_____

Question: Several pastors mentioned the importance of getting the right person in the right job within the church. What are tools that can assist with selection and management of staff and volunteers? How can you support your pastor in these critical decisions?

_____

_____

Action: What should the attitude of a church member be when he or she disagrees with one of the pastor's decisions? Look at 1 Peter 5:5 and Hebrews 13:17. Write out your commitment to publicly support your pastor's decisions (as long as they do not violate Scripture). When you disagree, seek to address the issue privately and positively with your pastor.

OPERATION SAVE OUR PASTORS · 31

Chapter 1 Notes

CHAPTER TWO

The Loneliest Profession

There are as many different types of Pastors as there are ice cream flavors, but one thing is for certain—they need our help. Anyone who's spent even a small amount of time will tell you that being in full-time ministry is one of the loneliest professions on God's green globe. No matter what you do, someone always thinks you could do better, or different, or more loud, or less loud ... the list goes on and on.[4]

If you have ever been surprised or offended by your pastor appearing rushed or uninterested in what you have to say, chances are that this is merely the tip of an unseen iceberg of stress.

Many pastors are in desperate need of a tool to help them deal with the pressures and isolation their job brings. Those of us who attend church, who listen to the sermon, and who appreciate the prayerful counsel of our local pastors do not fully understand the enormity of their role. When God calls someone for ministry, there is a sense of burden that could be overwhelming for many people.

How effective can a pastor be when they continuously experience an insurmountable amount of stress and pressure? McKenna and Eckard conducted an analysis in 2009 measuring the effectiveness of a pastor.[5] They did this by allowing the participating pastors to evaluate themselves in an interview in fourteen areas: "growing spiritually, meaningful worship, empowering leadership, internal experience of congregation (sharing faith), caring for youth and children, meeting spiritual demands of the congregation, attendance, membership, tithing, sense of belonging, participation in congregation, community involvement, following the 'golden rule' of leadership, and intentional leadership."

Maybe you're already starting to wonder how one person could be expected to excel in all these different ways. Of course, many of us have job descriptions that sound a little like this. An office manager, for example, may need to show a range of good leadership and administration skills. However, not many also have the responsibility of meeting the "spiritual demands" of those under them.

For those of us who are not pastors, our work lives are generally hidden from our brothers and sisters in church, and most of us can leave work behind on the weekend. But a pastor's work life is lived in public. There is nowhere to hide when things are difficult.

The Cost of Stress

While these fourteen areas are certainly linked with pastoral leadership, they give rise to some vital questions: What is the personal cost of achieving all of this? What happens when someone fails in one or more areas? Taking it a step further, what happens when a pastor experiences emotional exhaustion and can't carry on? Unfortunately, this is not unusual. In fact, I believe it is a widespread problem for pastors, especially those in the African American culture, to suffer mild to severe emotional exhaustion, commonly referred to as burnout.

Because pastors are human, the experience of burnout takes a toll on the individual pastor spiritually, emotionally, physically, and cognitively. Back in 1983, Ellison and Mattila noted that pastoral burnout stems from the following: "inordinate time demands, unrealistic expectations, sense of inadequacy, and fear of failure, loneliness, and spiritual dryness."[6]

Thirty-five years later, their findings are even more relevant. While no doubt some pastors can recover and return to ministry after suffering emotional exhaustion, today we see an increased percentage of church leaders preparing to throw in the towel due to the consuming demands of serving as pastor.

However, some pastors are brought to such a point of desperation that they don't merely leave the ministry—they end their life. In 1999, Spaite concluded that pastors often encounter the "messiah complex," which is the urgent need to rescue others and offer salvation from the sins of this world. If the pastor does not feel effective in this area of their pastoral duties, it could lead them to feel emotionally isolated from others.[7]

When this happens, it leads to one of two things. Either the pastor ends up resigning from their pastoral duties, or they begin making unruly and thoughtless decisions for his or her life. Such decisions could include actions such as misusing alcohol or drugs, committing adultery, falling into domestic abuse, and even committing suicide. When it comes to suicide, it initially begins with suicidal thoughts. In the same article, Spaite gave some pertinent statistics that showed why the rate of suicide is relatively high in the pastoral profession.

One example is Pastor Isaac Hunter, the son of President Obama's onetime spiritual advisor. He committed suicide shortly after his resignation once it was released that he had engaged in an affair with his female assistant, even though he was married. His wife also reported a case against him regarding domestic violence. After resigning, he was described as erratic and unstable, and eventually this led him to commit suicide.[8]

Unfortunately, this has become a trend in the pastoral profession. An article on pastoral burnout in the *New York Times* (2010) stated that the pastoral profession, alongside medicine and law, has one of the top three suicide rates of all professions.[9]

When I read this, I was overwhelmed with a multitude of emotions. I was surprised that the pastoral profession was so high on the list of suicide rates. I was also overcome with a feeling of melancholy for those pastors who had taken their lives because they didn't know how to handle the pressures. And my heart broke for their families, who now have to navigate life without them. It was at this point that I believe God told me this book was absolutely necessary for the survival of pastors.

The *New York Times* article reported other disheartening statistics as well. Forty-five percent of the pastors in the study claimed to have endured burnout or depression to the point of taking a leave of absence. A significant 52 percent of them believed that their position as pastor was perilous to the well-being of their families. Forty-eight percent of these pastors shared that their marriages had ended in divorce. An overwhelming 75 percent of the pastors testified that they had stumbled upon stress so great that it caused them anguish, worry, fear, and depression. The article further stated that the rate of pastors exiting the ministry at that time (in 2010) was 1,500 per month. That's extreme!

It is no wonder that so many pastors commit suicide when you consider a study by the Schaeffer Institute, which reveals that 70 percent of pastors battled depression, 71 percent were extremely burned out, 80 percent said their job had negative effects on family, and 70 percent had no close friends.[10]

It is evident that pastors feel lonely and suffer from depression while seeking to obey God's call on their lives.

A Stressful Job

Most pastors would agree that the joys of pastoring a congregation are often mixed with a wide range of problems. We need to explore stress management in religious leadership because the situation is serious. The effects of stress are becoming more intense and widespread in today's society, and that includes pastors.

Any position of leadership is certainly demanding. That's why it is vital for pastors to be aware of the signs of stress in themselves and also put strategies in place for managing this stress. The fact that their role and calling come from God doesn't mean they won't suffer from a range of physical and psychological issues, including emotional exhaustion, overwork, fatigue, insomnia, depression, financial difficulties, and family problems.

When I set out to investigate this subject, I was astounded that very little research exists that describes the relationship between stress and the leadership roles of pastors. It wasn't a case of examining the evidence—there was no evidence! It seemed that the world was happily unaware of, or possibly turning a blind eye to, the difficulties experienced by so many who serve in this essential role.

Leadership and other relative factors, such as stress, job satisfaction, and leadership style, have all been researched extensively. Research on stress management within religious leadership, on the other hand, is minimal. I wanted to supply the missing data while responding to this pertinent issue.

For this reason, gaining research specifically to support my topic was a difficult task. However, I do believe that the results will bring comfort to those pastors who are struggling in their position. They are not alone!

It has been confirmed multiple times that being aware of how others are struggling and understanding what others do to cope successfully with the demands of the job are essential tools for pastors in their walk with Christ.

The Effects of Stress

What does stress do to our bodies? According to a 2008 study by Mills, Reiss, and Dombeck,

> Because of their effects on the immune system, stress hormones impact the development and severity of many different diseases and bodily systems. In some instances, stress causes existing conditions to worsen. In other cases, stress seems to be a major factor creating vulnerability to developing new conditions in the first place.[11]

In the following chapters, we'll be taking a look at the role of the pastor and a range of issues facing pastors today, drawing on what our interviewees had to say in each case. You can compare their comments on each issue in the Appendix.

Later we'll turn our attention to practical strategies to help pastors cope with stress and suggest ways to lighten their workload.

Because emotional stress can have a negative effect on our health, the importance of this subject can't be overstated if the Church is to continue to spread the gospel and make disciples in the twenty-first century. We need our pastors, and we need them to enjoy all the blessings of physical and emotional well-being. To address this issue, we must first understand how and why pastors are facing such difficulty in their ministry role. As we uncover what the research reveals, pastors will be better equipped to stay healthy as they edify the Body of

Christ and their congregations will be better able to life them up.

WORKBOOK

Chapter 2 Questions

Question: What are some of the unique stressors that pastors face? What problems can result from long-term, unchecked stress?

_____

_____

_____

_____

_____

_____

_____

_____

_____

_____

_____

Question: What is a "messiah complex" in ministry? What are some symptoms that a pastor is operating under a messiah complex? How does this mindset contradict the scriptural role of a pastor (see Ephesians 4:11–14).

_____

_____

_____

_____

_____

_____

_____

_____

_____

_____

Question: Why do you think the suicide rate among pastors is disturbingly high? Where can a pastor who has "fallen from grace" find hope and help—or what resources need to be developed for this purpose?

_____

_____

_____

_____

_____

_____

_____

_____

_____

_____

_____

_____

Action: Send your pastor a note or email of appreciation. Be sure to use this only to express gratitude, not to discuss differences.

Chapter 2 Notes

CHAPTER THREE

Challenges and Stressors Pastors Face Daily

The research outlined in chapter 2 reveals that pastors are under an extreme amount of stress, which can lead to depression and even suicide. When I interviewed the pastors in my study, I asked each one to identify the aspects of the job that tend to be the most stressful. What puts them under pressure the most? Where does this pressure come from? Understanding the source of their stress is the first step to overcoming the burnout that so many pastors face.

The list of stressors mentioned during interviews was so extensive and covered such a range of topics that it took six tables to list them! Based on the number and length of content in Tables 1 through 6 (see Appendix), it is safe to say that Baptist church pastors experience emotional stress that is directly related to their pastoral role.

Aspects of the job that lead to stress were split into different categories. These are given in more detail in the Appendix, but let's take a broad look at each category in turn.

Stressors from Within and Without

The first category (see Table 1) lists some of the pressures that pastors confront, both from within themselves and from external forces. These pressures range from unfounded accusations against religious entities at large, as society casts about for someone or something to blame for present-day woes, to governmental interference and pressure. They also include the need for each pastor to understand the unique culture of his church as he strives to be a source of continual inspiration.

Then there are the forces of modernity, including social media, as church leaders struggle to make church practices, along with unwilling congregants, more contemporary. Taking all these factors together, we see what a wide range of stressors pastors must cope with.

Stressors from the Congregation

The second category of stress factors comes from the congregation. Pastors are called to shepherd their flock, yet the flock—the church members themselves—can create a considerable number of stressors. (See Table 2 in the Appendix for more details.)

These factors include a growing unwillingness in some groups to attend church for worship. Some church members feel this isn't necessary, and they don't attend regularly. Others are resistant to growth, both personally as individuals and when the church strives to become or stay contemporary.

Along these lines, stressors from church members also include widespread shirking of personal and spiritual responsibility. Where the pastor doesn't seem to inspire dedication, commitment, and renewal, he may not only feel discouraged, but also experience a deep sense of failure.

Another source of stress is bickering among the members. Pastor Summers told me, "God forbid that Deacon Jones says something Sister Smith didn't like; now you've got to deal with that conflict as well. You've got folks who want to cuss each other out, you got folks who want to fight one another because 'I didn't like the way she looked at me in the choir.'"

Bickering corresponds to another source of stress, which stems from the myriad of people that comprise a congregation—all of different ages, walks of life, experiences, and attitudes—all of which the pastor must somehow comprehend and shepherd.

Finally, pastors feel stress from the unrealistic expectations of their church members. People often expect them to be available 24/7, with no time off, no private life, and no personal concerns.

Pastor Harris provided a good example of the competing demands of the pastoral calling:

> I think that one of the biggest challenges—let me give you three. I think that number one is unrealistic expec-

tations from the congregation. When I say that, [I mean that] a lot of times, the expectations that the congregation has of the pastor are unreal. They expect the pastor to be everywhere at the same time, and it's not that they don't care.

For instance, I have a situation—since we're talking—I had a situation about a month ago where I needed a much-needed vacation. It was cut short.

When I got back that morning my stepdad—I was in the emergency room with him and my grieving mother. At the same time, another member died, and so I was calling them, praying for them, trying to take care of my family, and then someone called, complaining that I did not spend adequate time with the other member.

So, there are times when I think that the congregation does not realize that I'm human, that I have emotions, I have needs like everyone else. I think that unrealistic expectation on the pastor is the number-one thing.

In short, pastors must cope with a range of "people problems," both spiritual and practical. Their congregations come to them seeking advice, comfort, mediation, and support for a myriad of other needs.

The Pressures of Involvement

Thirdly, there is the constant stream of activities in and around the church that require the pastor's involvement. Pastors' comments on the need to be involved with the congregation revealed that they each engage in varying levels, but they all agreed that being involved means being pulled in a thousand different directions. Table 4 lists some of those directions that compete for the pastor's time.

It seems that pastors must balance stressors ranging from burnout to others placing a messiah complex upon them—and, it would appear, all without sufficient support or encouragement.

Involvement is expected, perhaps even accepted as a given. It also seems that very few people say, "Thank you for all your work, Pastor," or if they do, they don't say thank you often enough. Maybe we need to remember that pastors are human and that they appreciate kind and encouraging words as much as anyone else.

Stressors from the Family

The fourth category comes from those closest to the pastor. Table 3 in the Appendix lists the stress factors that involve the pastors' wives and children.

Family-related stressors have many dimensions. The primary stressor is the wholesale loss of privacy, a stress that the entire family shares. They also include the loss of time spent as a family, because plans with the pastor as dad or husband often give way to the needs of the church.

Another aspect involves the personal freedom of family members, who, as part of the pastor's family, are expected to be paragons of virtue and avoid all types of behavior that could incite criticism. This suggests that pastors must cope with considerable pressures from within the family, and other family members often endure plenty of pressure, too.

Stressors from the Loss of a Personal Life

We've already seen how the loss of privacy in the family is a contributing factor to the pastor's stress levels. Above and beyond family-related stressors, however, another source of stress is the loss of a pastor's personal life. When this aspect is left undernourished, it makes it very difficult for him to provide that continual source of creativity and inspiration that parishioners expect, or perhaps even demand.

Table 5 lists a number of stressors stemming from the loss of a personal life. These include "living in a fishbowl"—the pressure of consistently exhibiting upstanding behavior, as well as the considerable pressures of constant scrutiny and the judgment of others.

They also touch on the striving for public success in the pulpit at the cost of private failure at home. They include the loss of personal associates, all of whom are scrutinized by the attentive congregation that is keen to ensure their pastor is a role model of purity in word and deed.

In total, the stressors listed in Table 5 make it clear that pastors oftentimes feel trapped under the weight of being continually monitored by their congregations.

Social Media as a Stressor

On the topic of the pastor's loss of a personal life, Pastor Summers went into detail about the negative role of social media. His comment is shown below in its entirety, as it reveals both the passion of the interviews that were conducted and the gravity of the situation when "life in the fishbowl" takes on international but also anonymous proportions.

> The one thing that is new and has become a real problem for the church is social media. Social media is the biggest downfall of the modern Church. [I say this] because years ago, if there was something going on, people had to call one another and then they would only call people in their circle. Things that happened within the church, for the most part, stayed within the church, or at least the church community. Now you have people who just post things, and [both] saved and unsaved people read their posts. Some people spread the gossip among one another and you don't even have to call anybody and say, "Did you see so and so's post?" All they do is repost it or screenshot it to somebody. And for unsaved people, they literally say, "If that's what you all are doing in the Church, I don't want no part of that." So social media can be a gift to the Body of Christ. But rather than becoming a gift to the Body of Christ, it has become one of our biggest issues. [For example], people come to choir rehearsal and something happens in choir rehearsal and it ain't even nothing big, but the one member that didn't come to choir rehearsal heard about it, and then it gets on Facebook or something … now you've got a mess in the church over something that somebody sat in their living room and just typed on a keyboard or typed in their phone.

> You know, it used to take hours to call six or seven people and so … church gossip only [reached] so many people…. Now if you've got 400 friends on Facebook, you get to spread church gossip in a matter of seconds.

> So, social media is absolutely, beyond a shadow of a doubt, the biggest modern-day challenge to the church. I'm an educator in addition to being pastor, and even in the schools, people don't bully like they used to. Now they sit at home and they do it online….

So, we literally have to pay people—pay staff—to monitor social media to see what the day is going to look like, the next day of school. And the same thing happens in church. I can't tell you how many phone calls I've gotten over the years about something that somebody posted, or somebody come into my office saying, "Pastor, did you see this? This is what somebody put out there." Now I've got to deal with this because you know even older people, they're not on social media for the most part, but they hear about that. Their grandchildren come and show them, "Oh, look at what so-and-so put on there."

It's absolutely crazy. You've got people who monitor.... That's why I got off Facebook, because I didn't realize that my members were monitoring my page. And I didn't even post, I haven't been on Facebook for three years, but I didn't even post anything like that, because they will literally monitor my page.

When I was married, they monitored my wife's page. When we were going through our divorce, they literally just stayed on her page. And ... whatever she put out there, they would screenshot it to everybody else.

It's like social media is Satan to the church. It's Satan, it is. It could be used in so many marvelous ways, you could literally ... take the Word of God and post that on your page and share that with the others. But instead of sharing the Word with others, we share foolishness.

I've got members who sit outside my church after service and take selfies or group shots and post it on the internet. And it's like, okay, first of all, you just got out of the service of the Lord, why are you all taking pictures? And you don't take pictures on the day that you're dressed nicely. You take pictures on the day that everybody in the group is dressed like a thug. But that's the day you take pictures and you immediately post it, like it's nothing.

That's what I mean about this whole social media 24-hour news cycle that's going on. It makes everything seem so much worse, but it's not. You've always had the alcoholics, but didn't nobody know about it, because nobody was taking pictures. You've always had philandering ministers, but nobody knew about it, because nobody was taking pictures, nobody was posting nothing. His wife knew about it, and when he got home, she'd cuss him out. He'd cry, promise not to do it again, then start all over.

Not now. Now, if you see Reverend so-and-so at the restaurant with a woman, you take a picture of his car, take a picture of him in there with the woman, and then all 400 of your Facebook friends now have an instant picture of the pastor and another woman.

You know social media, I've got to tell you, I can go on all into the night about social media, I really can. I know you don't have that kind of time.

Without going into the animated detail about social media that Pastor Summers provided, Pastor Dwight also mentioned social media as part and parcel of larger societal ills: "Social media. The way people portray pastors in the movies. How people view religion now. Of course, our liberalness. Society as a whole is lax. There's nothing fearsome. We don't fear anything."

In addition to these sources of stress, there are a significant amount of other stressors that stretch beyond these categories.

Additional Stressors

Several other stressors did not fall into neat categories but nonetheless represent other sources of pastoral anxiety and tension.

Pastor Steven pointed out that his church added pressure because it lacked adequate resources, essentially forcing him "to make bricks without straw. You're expected to do, in many cases, everything, but the resources are not there to get it done."

Pastor Dwight pointed out that there is no set schedule, which can lead to a sense of chaos and disorganization. A pastor without an organized schedule may lack focus and find himself rushing at the last minute and providing mediocre ministry to his congregation. Two pastors referred to material compensation. Pastor Summers commented, "None of us get paid for the work we do, none of us. None of us get paid for the amount of stress and strife. So, you're not even compensated for the stress and strain of what you do in the church." Pastor Steven admitted, "We took a pay cut to come here—a major one. My wife gave up her job for us to come here."

These are essential things pastors deal with on a daily basis, but they often remain unspoken. The expectations and amount of pressure these pastors face aren't reasonable and stretch beyond what any human should experience. Preaching the Word of God and leading the flock are difficult and comes with a weighty responsibility. This role is often accompanied by the stress factors contained in this chapter. However, many pastors feel overwhelmed and ill-equipped to cope with the stress that's encountered in ministry. The following chapter examines how a lack of coping strategies can lead to temptation.

WORKBOOK

Chapter 3 Questions

Question: What do you find to be the most unexpected stressor that pastors face? Why did this stressor surprise you?

_____

_____

_____

_____

_____

_____

_____

_____

_____

_____

Question: In what situations might you have contributed to your pastor's stress in a way that could have been avoided or handled differently? In the future, how will you address a similar situation?

_____

_____

_____

_____

_____

_____

_____

_____

_____

_____

Question: In what ways is social media potentially a detriment to the church and a cause of stress for the pastor? How can social media be used to further the ministry of the church? How can church members be wise and mature in their usage of social media?

_____

_____

_____

_____

_____

_____

_____

_____

_____

_____

_____

_____

Action: Make a list of the things you find stressful in your personal and work life. Compare that list with the stressors that pastors experience. What similarities do you see that will help you be more compassionate for what your pastor is experiencing? Write out any insights this exercise brings to light for you.

_____

_____

_____

_____

_____

_____

_____

_____

_____

Chapter 3 Notes

CHAPTER FOUR

Coping with Stress

The next area I wanted to explore was about coping mechanisms. How do pastors handle the stressful situations they've mentioned? A few of the pastors followed up their commentary on their biggest challenges with voluntary explanations of how they cope with them.

Lack of Outlets

Pastors are, after all, only human, and under stress their minds and bodies react in very human ways. Pastor Steven said, "If we don't get outlets [for this stress], we major in what I call 'the dark arts.'"

When Pastor Steven says, "the dark arts," he is referring to the temptations that can arise when pastors seek to self-medicate their stress with unhealthy, and even sinful, behavior.

Problems mentioned here include a temptation to turn to alcohol or drugs to relieve the tension. Pastor Dwight said, "People will drive you to drink, drugs, or whatever—to your vices—to the point you're not thinking."

Pastor Jake pointed out that a lack of professional support means people can reach a breaking point: "It's incredibly important to know that there's a lot of pastors who are hurting, a lot of personal issues and things. Because we all can get the private demons sometimes to manifest and [get] attacked more than anybody else.... Unfortunately, pastors don't have a place to go to really be transparent and get help."

The best way to sum up the wide range of challenges they face is with a quote from Pastor Trenton: "Nobody knows what a pastor goes through but another pastor."

Pastor Steven warned of the dangers of the hero complex, or the messiah complex—the lure of trying to be the superhuman pastor who does it all:

> In the African American context, one of the dangers is the hero complex—the savior complex. We put that pressure on ourselves, where we got to do everything. We're the first to get there. We're the last to leave.
>
> We give everything to the church, and there's not enough for wife, husband, children. And we raise children who hate God—or they hate the God we showed them, the God that took Daddy from them or the God that took Mom from them. The expectation is that we have to do everything. Living in a fishbowl for the family is a big one.

Pastor Steven coped with these temptations by surrounding himself with adequate staff, a useful trick he picked up in the army:

> For me, the answer is staff. That's my motto. That's my experience. The military helped me quite a bit with this. I was an officer in the army for eight years, so I understand delegation, levels of authority, level of responsibility, not trying to do everything. You do what's in your wheelhouse. You do what's in your expertise level, and you stay there.
>
> You empower and release authority and responsibility to people who can be trusted, but also people who have the acumen and the capacity for a particular area.
>
> So, for me, I thank God for that experience because it has saved my life. We've quadrupled in three years. We've gone from 300 to over 1,300, and trying to do that alone ... man. You all would be wheeling me out of here!

Pastor Paul started by summarizing the outcome of various challenges succinctly: "Stress. Stress. Fatigue. Depression." But he ended loquaciously:

> A lot of pastors are sensitive in nature, and they desire that status quo kind of ministry. You know, everybody's not going to have a church like, you know, Friendship West in Dallas, one of the larger African American churches in the nation. And everybody's not going to have that. Some pastors stress themselves out thinking that they're failing because they don't grow to that level. And you know [because of all of the competing pressures], you have to have a clear sense of who you are and where you are and what you're going to be.
>
> And a lot of times there's demographics. You may have experienced already in your, I'd call it, short time in the

South. People are more inclined to go to church in the South en masse, you know what I'm saying? A small church in the South is probably 500 to 1000 in most cases. A mega church in the South is, you know, 60, 70 thousand. Up here [in Chicago], a megachurch here [has only] got two or three thousand members, and you're an anomaly, there's a very few. There are thousand-member churches all over Tennessee, just on average, on any given Sunday. So a lot of pastors stress themselves out trying to meet that number.

You know, I have a saying: Don't get caught up in your seating capacity. Be more concerned about your ascending capacity—not what comes in your church but what goes out of it every week.

Along somewhat similar lines, Pastor Harris thought that the biggest challenge is "unrealistic expectations from the congregation." He went on to list three other major challenges, the first of which corresponds to a loss of one's social circle. He gave a strong warning to watch whom you spend time with while you are living in the aforementioned fishbowl. He recommended coping by developing a mystique with your parishioners:

I think there is a great deal of loneliness in leadership. You cannot extend yourself to everyone and you cannot, you know, you have to maintain a sense of—I'm trying to think of a good word for it. You have to be very careful with the friendships that you maintain, that they don't overstep the line, number one, and that it does not move you into a place of commonality.

And when I say commonality, I think that there should be somewhat of a mystique, some sense of mystique, where he's [more] distinguishable as a pastor rather than fitting in with the crowd and cliques.

I think that you can become too familiar. You can cross a line with members, and when you cross that line with members, you lose respect. And so I think there should be a mystique a pastor should have. It might sound old and fogey, but I think there's a sense of mystique or mystery about a pastor that should remain. I don't think that the pastor should become too common with the congregants. That doesn't mean he doesn't check on them, make sure they're doing fine, doing well. I'm talking about, if the member is having a party, you don't show up and hang out.

I was born in the church. When I was in seminary, they said one of those challenges is that familiarity breeds contempt, and so because when I grew up I hung out with some of them, it's hard for them to kind of transpose the picture [of me] from friend to pastor.

As for Pastor Harris's third biggest challenge: "…I would say resistance from the congregation to [grow up because they are] more comfortable in a position of mediocrity. The reason I say that is because there is a group of young and old that have joined church under me, that are more progressive than, say, the people that were here under my granddad. I'm a transitional pastor. I'm succeeding my grandfather. The newer people that have come in the last thirteen years under my leadership, they're more progressive than the older membership, whether young or old. They're a lot more comfortable with the person that's doing that."

This situation puts Pastor Harris in a challenging situation of having to balance the dynamics of a congregation that is mixed with conservative and progressive members. The reality is, he can't please everyone. So trying to find that balance is difficult while always leaving some members unsatisfied.

As a final challenge, Pastor Harris spoke of how pastors avoid controversial subjects and therefore deliver shallow messages that don't get to the deep issues dealt with in the Word of God. This corresponds to his personal theme of love of knowledge, which he promoted in many aspects of his commentary.

> Number four, I think that pastors do not preach the Word. I think that is detrimental to the growth of the church. You have to dig deeper into the Word, particularly with your generation because I did a lot of research—Lifeway magazine talks about a lot of your generation's leaders because pastors are doing what I like to call surface preaching. They don't do any deep-sea diving.

> They don't deal with the hot issues like gay marriage or same-sex marriage or homosexuality—those are the hot potatoes right there. And I think that has to be addressed from the pulpit, especially in this generation because it's so vivid. So, I think that spiritual, Biblical preaching that relates to modern-day issues, where pastors don't do that I think it's detrimental to the growth of the church.

Pastor Smithson had a very different kind of challenge, but it may be linked to the lack of deep spiritual study: "greed." When I prompted him to explain, he said pastors too often heed the temptation to forget their calling:

> Explain it? We live in a culture where you can never have enough, where we live based on pleasure, profit,

and production. Profit and production—more than really the call and the purpose—whereas [the call and purpose] used to be the primary objective.

The purpose becomes the springboard for really worldly pleasures. A lot of pastors fall into the trap of numbers or luxury items or nothing else, just the power of being a pastor. We lose sight of the purpose that we're actually hired by God to do a job, holy work.

Like Pastor Harris, Pastor Trenton listed several challenges. One had to do with nourishing the shepherd in return for his good works. He smoothly combined the challenge with advice for coping with it. Then he ushered in the metaphor of pastoring as parenting.

The biggest challenge, I believe, that's facing pastors today is encouragement. We don't receive the encouragement that we need. I'm fortunate, just as well as numerous others that you're going to talk to because they're out of our core group, and we have a bond. We have a—I'm trying to think of the right word. We have this bond that we come together weekly to encourage one another, you know, because, see, when you're out here, you know, and you're having those struggles that the people are not listening. Again, just like any parent, when the people are not listening and they're not doing what they need to be doing to obtain the fullness of life, then you become discouraged, because of the fact that you're saying, "Well, is it me? Am I doing all I can do?"

It becomes very stressful. But then, by the same token, again, like any parent, when you know that you are doing something and you're getting upset or, again, impatient, because you want the best for your children, see? So, it's, you know, one of those things that we always say among ourselves is that nobody knows what a pastor goes through but another pastor.

But with a pastor, we all have the same struggles out here because there's only one God. So if we're serving Him the way that we should be, then we're going to have those struggles, and we have to encourage one another.

Pastor Wright referred to unrealistic expectations from the congregation when he said that "every time something takes place in society, it's not the pastors and the church that is at blame," but they get blamed anyway:

Some of the biggest challenges I'd say facing pastors today is that I feel as though everything that seems to take place in society, there's always a blame, it seems, put first on the pulpit.

I just faced an issue the other day with a young man that I've known his whole life. He was saying that the Church and pastors don't do anything but take money from people, but when you need financial help, the Church doesn't help anyone. But that's not true.

The Church is not a bank. It is not a loan institution where you can go get a loan. But the church has helped people in so many different aspects and financially, too. Some churches have financing, too, but that's one of the challenges.

Pastor Wright had other examples of how the Church is unfairly blamed for societal ills or issues. His final comment harkened back to the pressures of involvement (see Table 8):

And they tend to do that [blame the Church] often, from homosexuality to killings in the street, with our young men who are going in and out of prisons as well as murdering one another. They put that right on the Church, right in our laps. So, we always face the challenge socially.

It's as if they want us to take over their homes, you know. We can't. We can only speak a word to them, and hopefully, like you were saying, it will inspire them. And then as they're inspired, then it can make the difference in whatever issue that they're dealing with and in their everyday walk, especially in this life that we're living—instead of just dropping everything in laps and saying it's the church's fault. The pastors aren't doing—they're not doing that.

And little do they know the pastor is doing quite a bit. He's praying constantly for them and, you know, all the way to visiting the sick, coming to the prisons to visit their relatives, and making calls and things like that, checking up on them, and—I mean, the pastor is always involved. I'll say and put it like this, I try to stay involved.

In contrast to Pastor Wright's example of congregants who expect more from the Church, Pastor Lowe's challenge was grappling with those who want less of the Church: "The biggest challenges, I feel, facing pastors today would be a falling away from or going away from corporate worship, a gathering of people." He went on to explain that societal changes have reduced the importance of attending church services, because there seems to be other ways to accomplish spirituality: "We're living in a time now actually—I feel that everyone feels as if they can connect to God and tune in to God on their own. So, there is no need for coming together with other believers." This attitude is, of course, a death knell for any church.

Pastor Blake also said one of his challenges was getting congregants to commit, but also to support the Church:

> Well, probably number one is commitment, is a big one, getting people to commit, it's a huge one. There's a theory I call, "how to close the back door." It's basically how to keep the people that you get: They come in the front door, but they go out the back door! Now, that's a big one.
>
> Giving, of course, is always a big one. That's a big one. And probably, you know for the pastor himself individually, balancing church and personal [life] is a big challenge.

Pastor Jake also thought a tremendous challenge for a pastor was to balance his calling and his home life. Pastor West had even more to say about the precarious balance between a spiritual calling to serve and a pastor's home life, and he did not mince words:

> Biggest challenges for the pastors? I would say, one is carnality, also the lack of I would say, a lack of commitment from the [flock]. And then of course we have to deal with the government seeking to dictate how the church moves.
>
> No one is perfect, and we can feel that and so therefore we all sin every day, but carnality to the point where ... it seems as if church is not taken as seriously as it once was. For some the Sunday morning worship experience is more a thing to do, a ritual, so it's assembly.

In the face of such challenges, pastors are often overwhelmed and lack outlets to cope with their stress.

However, it doesn't have to be the reality. There is a better way. The last two chapter will explore how pastors can address these challenges in a healthy way, and how their congregations can help.

WORKBOOK

Chapter 4 Questions

Question: How is being a pastor often like being a parent? How can the struggles of parenthood help you to understand the stresses that your pastor faces?

Question: What do you think about the expectation of the pastor being involved in every aspect of the church vs. the pastor maintaining a level of "mystique" and not being overly familiar with his congregation? What would a balance between these two extremes look like?

_____

_____

_____

_____

_____

_____

_____

_____

_____

_____

Question: What "guardrails" should a healthy church have in place to help its pastor avoid burnout? What provisions should the church make to help if burnout does occur?

_____

_____

_____

Action: Examine your unspoken expectations of your pastor and write them down. Are there places and activities that you are involved in but would be upset if your pastor or his family did the same? Are there times when you think he has neglected a pastoral duty that you yourself could also have done but didn't (e.g. visiting someone in the hospital)? Review the list. Are your expectations fair, realistic, and biblical? Are you looking to your pastor to meet needs that only Jesus can meet? In large letters over your list of expectations, write the word "GRACE."

OPERATION SAVE OUR PASTORS · 73

Chapter 4 Notes

CHAPTER FIVE

What Every Pastor Needs to Know

Having heard from all of our pastors, what have we learned? From their comments, it is clear that those in Church leadership—generally sincere, hardworking men and women of God, who fully understand the privilege and responsibilities of their role—are struggling to cope with the physical, emotional, and spiritual pressures they face.

What can be done to help them? Before we discuss what churches can do to support their pastors, let's uncover what pastors can do to help themselves.

Every Pastor Needs a Pastor

I have taught in a public-school system for five years. I know how it feels to have a lack of support from family and friends who are not, or have never been, in a teaching position. It can be very lonely when it seems as though no one can comprehend the scale of what you're going through on a daily basis.

I often receive the typical phrases of encouragement such as: "You'll be all right," "It's only temporary," and "I'm praying for you." Although these are much appreciated, it somehow doesn't seem like sufficient support. We all need someone who can truly understand and identify with our daily struggles, whatever our walk is in life. That's why, with all that educators face on a consistent basis, we mentor and look to one another to encourage and offer advice when there is a need.

I mention this experience because I can only begin to imagine what it would feel like to be the pastor of any congregation, small or large, where the pressures are more wide-ranging and continue into the evenings and weekends, with no long vacations in sight.

When I planned the interviews with pastors that I needed for my dissertation, I asked each pastor a total of ten open-ended questions. I expected each interview to take around 30 to 45 minutes, but most of my interviews lasted far longer than I'd imagined.

I learned several things from this experience. One of the lessons learned was that pastors can really talk! Most of them went on and on like the Energizer bunny. This led me to my next observation, which some of them confirmed: Pastors generally have no one to talk to when it comes to venting about their duties and how they really feel about their vocations. No wonder they seized the opportunity to share, frankly and anonymously, with me what was on their minds.

I have heard it said that "every pastor needs a pastor" all my life. But when I was a child, I never fully understood what it meant. Why would a pastor, of all people, need to have a pastor? I mean, isn't he already the boss? I had to grow up spiritually and see certain things to put this aphorism into perspective.

The pastor of the pastor serves as a mentor. This is often someone who has been in his or her own pastoral position for some time, at least fifteen to twenty years. This pastor has seen the celebrations and downfalls of the Church as well as those of other leaders. They have most likely experienced such ups and downs themselves, giving them the wisdom and empathy needed to help others facing similar issues. This would be the ideal person to support a new or younger pastor in the ministry.

I certainly believe that many of the public failures of pastors seen in the media could be avoided or mitigated if ministers in the Church had a support system with meaningful substance. This support system would need to be made up of people who were not afraid to be brutally honest. The pastor of the pastor would serve as an advisor, whose advice given would assist the pastor with making decisions that would not lead to public failures or embarrassment. Anyone serving in such a support role would also pray with and for the appointed pastor whom they mentored.

I met up for coffee with three of my mentor pastors in Chicago one day, and we discussed various aspects of pastoral leadership. One of my questions for them was: "What is your idea of a model pastor? What qualities should this person possess?" They provided a wealth of responses, as they had all themselves completed the process of recruiting a pastor to work with them.

Interestingly, all of them had spent most, if not all, of their childhoods in their current churches. Once their predecessors passed away, it was their responsibility to search for a new senior pastor to work with and mentor them.

When asked about the qualities they would look for, this is what they said:

> Someone who is spiritually connected. This person must have the ability and sensitivity to hear the voice of God.
>
> Someone who has a respectable work ethic. He or she must be able to inspire their "son" or "daughter" in the ministry to develop a well-rounded work ethic with both pastoral work and administration.
>
> As I stated before, this person must not be afraid to correct their mentee when they are treading down the wrong path.
>
> Someone who is cultivating their congregation and it is evident.
>
> Someone who is approachable and accessible.
>
> Someone who encourages progression in the ministry.

When I asked my mentor pastors how they selected another pastor for their churches, they told me that they usually narrowed it down to a few prospects who had the characteristics listed above, and then they went to God in prayer.

Young pastors trying to choose someone to serve with them should be careful not to select a pastor simply because he is popular. The "popular pastor" usually has a large congregation, which may make him an appealing choice, but the young pastor must be certain that this is the one God wants to lead him or her. One key point is to ensure that the newcomer sees eye to eye on vital issues, including setting priorities for the ministry.

Family Must Be a Priority

When it comes to setting priorities, I have often heard the saying among Christians that the order should be, "God, family, then Church." This states that God will always be first, that family should come after that, and then the Church should follow in order of importance. But how often does this really happen for pastors?

It can be extremely challenging for pastors to maintain this order of priorities. The demands of the Church can be overwhelming, to say the least, and it's not easy to guarantee a pastor's family's place on the list.

Faced with a full schedule of church activities, not to mention the various other duties of a pastor, how much time is left for the family? Very little, unfortunately. With the arduous tasks of a pastoral position, spouses and children are often neglected.

I want to offer some suggestions here to pastors who believe that the Church should come before their families. You may not realize it, but families suffer greatly under the pressures of having a pastor as the head of their household.

Growing up in the church as I did, I often witnessed the pastors' wives being the sole caretakers of the family—handling all circumstances related to their family on her own. This was expected by everyone, and yet this situation is not right in most cases. Men have a responsibility to care for their families. They need to be present for their wives and children in large and small ways.

I truly believe that pastors' wives also have to be called, because it can definitely be a difficult and stressful role, and the struggle can be intense. They often have to deal with not only their families, but also the church itself. They have to keep their husbands grounded and levelheaded. They have to demonstrate their support, even when they don't agree with what is going on.

Now, I am not speaking for all first ladies of churches. Some of these women have exceptional experiences—they have not faced as steep of a struggle to gain the respect of the church—but I am certain that this is not everyone's testimony. Just as I advocate for pastors, I advocate for their wives and children.

Some of you may be wondering why I believe that the family should come after a pastor's personal relationship with God but before the needs of his congregation. After all, it's the pastor's job. He is being paid for it. He is supposed to do this and that. It's what he signed up for. I get it.

On the other hand, we need to ask if this approach is sustainable. The "Church first" mentality is what causes many pastors to experience burnout and walk away from the pulpit. Yes, the congregation depends heavily on the pastor for spiritual support and guidance. But on whom does the pastor's family depend? The pastor also needs the love and support of his family to better fulfill his calling. While the congregation is often busy complaining about every decision, big or small, that the pastor makes, his family needs to keep him grounded and reassured of their love to help him carry on.

Even worse than the pressure placed on pastors and their wives is the effect of the pastorate on the children. It's not easy being a pastor's kid. The assumption of the rebellious son or daughter of a pastor—"Oh, you're the pastor's kid, so you must be bad"—is a commonplace in some churches and communities. How can these young men women develop their own identities when other people make such insensitive generalizations?

I believe that once a pastor embeds in his mind the idea that family comes after God and before the Church, he will be more successful. It will release a lot of the pressure, give him more time off to unwind and rejuvenate, and help him reestablish his identity as a husband and a parent. He will have the support he needs, and the church will have a more balanced, more well-rounded, and stronger leader.

It takes a certain level of maturity to have this mindset, however. This is why it is important that, when it comes to finding a new leader, a young pastor selects someone who feels the same way.

Pastors should ensure that date nights with their wives are consistent. They should ensure that time with their families is sacrosanct. In order for the pastor to have the support and peace of mind he needs from his home life, he must choose to prioritize his family.

Use Discernment with Your Circle of Friends

Besides his family, a pastor must be vigilant about whom he allows into his personal space. This doesn't mean that a pastor should go alone and never get close to anyone. Having a circle of intimate friends can be a great support. They should be able to offer advice when there is discouragement. The pastor should be able to confide in them, bearing in mind, of course, the need for confidentiality where appropriate. This could assist pastors with dealing with their stress more openly, because they would be comfortable enough to share what is bothering them, and with avoiding the unhealthy sense of isolation that can come with a leadership position.

However, it is imperative that a pastor heeds the voice of God when it comes to considering someone as a consistent member of his circle of friends. Forcing something against God's will or trying to maintain a relationship that God wants to remove can lead to destruction in a pastor's personal life and ministry.

There is a popular television show, *Greenleaf*, about the life of a pastor and his family. In one episode, the married pastor began to spend time with a seductress. She knew how to lure him out to restaurants, doctors' offices, and even a hotel.[12]

This pastor failed to use his discernment with letting her into his personal space. Little did he know, but she was on the same side as his enemy.

Inappropriate or risky relationships are all too common when it comes to pastoral leadership. If pastors want the respect and trust of their flock, they must present themselves as leaders by carefully selecting their friends.

Be Open to Leisure

With the number of responsibilities pastors carry as leaders in the Church, the idea of taking a vacation may seem overwhelming or impossible. However, relaxing time away from the communities they serve and the daily barrage of demands is exactly what they need every now and then.

I'm not talking about attending conventions and conferences, either. I mean a true family vacation. The pastor should arrange for others to handle anything that takes place while he is away so that his time off isn't interrupted by a stream of phone calls about issues he isn't present to fix.

Part of creating an opportunity for the pastor to take a vacation is making sure that the church can handle the pastor being away. If the pastor allows other ministers and deacons to work alongside him and fulfill some of the roles in his presence, the church will be better prepared to allow the pastor to take a break.

In addition to vacations, pastors should find some recreational activities or hobbies to use as a coping strategy. From sports and exercise to board games or just playing with the kids, having a hobby or interest outside of the church is a great way to relax and unwind.

Keeping all of this advice in mind can help to alleviate a pastor's stress levels, give him a more balanced life, and avoid common pitfalls. While majority of the responsibility falls on the pastor to manage his own mental, emotional, and spiritual health—there is a role that the church can play to alleviate some of the pastor's burden.

WORKBOOK

Chapter 5 Questions

Question: What qualities should a young pastor look for in a mentor? What are the benefits to every pastor having his or her own pastor?

Question: Why should the pastor's family come before his or her ministry? What are the consequences of putting ministry before family? What are some of the unique stressors that the pastor's spouse faces?

_____

_____

_____

_____

_____

_____

_____

_____

_____

_____

Question: Why is it important for the pastor to have leisure or recreational time removed from all church responsibilities? Other than vacations, how can this be accomplished? How can the church leadership help protect this personal time?

_____

_____

_____

Action: Plan a way to bless your pastor's family. Some ideas:

- Have them to your house for dinner.
- Pay for the pastor and his wife to have a date night (including money for a babysitter if that is a need).
- Give the pastor's wife a beautiful bouquet of flowers and a note of appreciation.
- Arrange for needed repair or upkeep to be done around their home and yard.

Chapter 5 Notes

CHAPTER SIX

What Every Congregation Needs to Know

Kathy was an elderly lady who visited her pastor one morning. When he was called out of his study briefly to deal with another issue, she browsed among his private papers on the desk and discovered that he was considering moving on to a different church.

Unable to say anything to the much-loved pastor without giving away that she had snooped and read his private mail, Kathy left the meeting and only told one other person. He, in turn, told everyone else.

The church members were devastated by the news—and hurt to learn it from someone other than the pastor. The pastor was devastated by the betrayal and by the damage it caused in the church.

Your pastor is a human being. That means he is entitled to the same consideration and respect as any other person. Unfortunately, not everyone seems to realize this.

As previously mentioned, I have been in the church all my life. I have witnessed how people respond to the pastor when they agree with him. I have witnessed how people respond to their pastor when they do not agree. I have even witnessed people bashing their own pastor to others outside of the church. This is devastating, and unfortunately it is even more common today than when I was a child.

People should understand that sharing negative opinions about their pastor is detrimental to the pastor as a person, as well as to the health and cultivation of the church. My aim in this chapter is not to point the finger of blame, but to help congregations understand how they can so easily add to their pastor's burdens and what they can do to be a blessing instead. I pray that this advice will have an impact on the expectations Christians have of their pastors.

Pastors Are People

First of all, we need to remember that our pastor is human. He is not God, which means that he is not perfect. All of us, as human beings, have to deal with the sin nature. We all make mistakes and poor decisions. While pastors, like all Christians, should strive to live according to God's will, expecting a pastor never to err places unrealistic, unfair, and unsustainable expectations on him. Instead, we should extend to him the grace that God so generously extends to us.

Next, we need to understand that our pastor is our pastor—and that's it. He is not our husband or our father, and he is not at our beck and call. If every church member expects the pastor to be everything to them, then he is pulled in too many directions. While our pastor deserves our respect, he is not superhuman. He can't be everywhere at once or even in two places at once.

I believe it's time to readjust our expectations of what we think a pastor should and should not do. Who are we to set these standards? God is the only One who should be guiding the pastor as he leads his flock. We need to step back and consider the pressure we place on our pastor and the toll that our demands take on his health, his family, and his ability to do the work God has called him to do.

Respect the Position

In some cases, a pastor serves in the same church he attended when he was growing up. It can be difficult to establish authority over people who knew you in your awkward or mischievous years, perhaps even when you took a wrong path instead of following Christ. In order for a pastor to lead his congregation in the way God has called him to do, the church members must respect his position. Even if we used to call the pastor by his childhood nickname, once he bears the title "pastor," we must acknowledge his authority as shepherd of the flock. Otherwise, we risk diminishing the messages God wills to deliver to us through him, and our spiritual growth will suffer.

While we are on the subject of respect, that also goes for the pastor's family. A pastor's wife and children are an important entity of the Church, and they deserve to be honored on anniversaries and pastoral appreciation days. Often they sacrifice the opportunity to be a complete family unit so that their husband and father can fulfill his duties to the Church.

That said, we need to understand that the pastor was called to the ministry, but the same may not apply to his children. Don't push the pastor's children to follow in his footsteps. Allow them to grow up without that added pressure and don't pass judgment on them just because they are the "first children" of your church.

As mentioned earlier, Pastor Steven put it this way: "We raise children who hate God—or they hate the God we showed them—the God who took Daddy from them, or the God who took Mom from them." Let's make sure the pastor's kids don't reject God because of the church their father leads.

Advocate for Your Pastor

I was a huge fan of the NBA star Derrick Rose for a long time. Derrick Rose was a kid from Chicago (Englewood, to be exact), and he attended the University of Memphis before he was drafted to the Chicago Bulls. I followed his career closely. D. Rose, as fans affectionately call him, has suffered several injuries throughout his career. This was hard enough for him, but in addition, he received a great backlash from the public, as though the injuries were his fault.

Anytime someone spoke ill of him, I was quick to defend him as if I knew him personally. I would actually get angry with people. (Thank God that I have been delivered from this attitude!) My point is that I was an advocate for him while he was healthy and when he was injured.

Within the Church, I have seen people be advocates for their pastors, but I have also seen people trash their pastors. Pastors require support, especially from their congregation.

As we have seen, pastors have a large number of responsibilities, from preparing and delivering weekly sermons and Bible study lessons, to facilitating meetings and juggling administrative duties, to managing finances, to directing and participating in church activities and ministries, to visiting those in hospitals and prisons, to conducting weddings, baptisms, dedications, and funerals—and the list goes on.

God has given each pastor a vision, and it's an enormous task to bring that vision to fruition. Instead of thinking about what your pastor might be doing wrong, ask God to show you how you can better support the person He has called to shepherd His Church.

Go to the throne of God on behalf of your pastor on a regular basis and be sure to contribute to your church's ministry by giving of your time and money. Fast for your pastor, asking God to continue to cultivate his ministry and give him wisdom to fulfill the vision. If people prayed for and gave to their pastors more than they gossiped and spread negativity about them, then pastors—and the Church as a whole—would be in much better shape.

Take care of your pastor! God sent him to your church for a reason.

What Can I Do to Help?

Andy Vaughn has shared several practical suggestions to support your pastor[13]:

- Give encouragement. Say positive things about the church and thank your pastor for the work that he does.
- Listen to the sermon and provide (positive!) feedback afterward or ask questions.
- Volunteer to help out. Churches always need volunteers, so get involved and help relieve your pastor's workload.
- Offer to lead a Bible study in your home or church.
- Bring a friend to church with you.
- Use social media to build up, not destroy. What could you post this week to help support your pastor and see God's kingdom grow?
- Allow your pastor to rebuke you if necessary; it's part of his job.

As Andy Vaughn says, "The list could go on and on…. Anything you can do to let [your pastor] know that he is not alone and can rely on you is helpful indeed."[14]

If you're not sure how to start, or what that would look like practically in life—consider this story.

Randy's Story

This is love: not that we loved God, but that he loved us and sent his Son as an atoning sacrifice for our sins. Dear friends, since God so loved us, we also ought to love one another. No one has ever seen God; but if we love one another, God lives in us and his love is made complete in us.
—**1 John 4:10–12** (NIV)

So, how might this work in practice? Let's look at a case study.

Randy is a Baptist pastor who is married with three children. He has suffered two breakdowns, largely as a result of job-related stress.

After recovering from the second, more serious breakdown, Randy and his family moved back to his previous church, where a vacancy had arisen. From being senior pastor of a large downtown church with several thousand members, he switched to being the sole pastor of a church of maybe two hundred members in a quiet country town.

When discussing a possible return with the deacons, Randy was open about his mental health issues and the need to minimize stress as much as possible. The deacons, who knew him and had loved him for years, set out to put certain systems in place. Working with Randy and his wife, they sought to lighten the workload so he could concentrate on his remarkable gifts of teaching and preaching.

As well as the team of deacons, the church now has a part-time administrator, a youth worker, and a full-time pastoral assistant, who works with volunteers to pray with those in need, visit the sick and housebound, and generally serve as the go-to contact for the pastoral work of the church. There are also home groups to provide spiritual support, Bible study, and sharing among the members.

By encouraging people to seek and develop their spiritual gifts, the church leadership has enabled certain church members to preach at Sunday services. Randy is not expected to participate in every one of the many church activities or be available 24/7. When the pastor needs time off, the church continues to function smoothly.

As well as taking a regular day off a week, Randy and his family build frequent short breaks and vacations into his schedule. He continues to take medication, but it is the practical and loving support of his wife, family, and church that has really made the difference in his life.

From the church's point of view, by working with Randy they have gained not only a great teacher and leader with a focus on spiritual growth, but also an increased understanding of mental health issues and a desire to work together to support the pastor they love.

It's time to remember that the Church is a family, the Body of Christ. We all have a role to play within the Church and a duty to care for one another. We need to share godly love and grace with all of our Christian brothers and sisters, including our pastors, and come together to show that love to the world.

WORKBOOK

Chapter 6 Questions

Question: How can thoughtless gossip destroy a ministry?

Question: How do unrealistic expectations and pressures harm a pastor's children? Why are pastors' kids at extra risk of rejecting God?

Question: Is your church overall an encouraging or discouraging place for your pastor to serve? Evaluate the church atmosphere and consider if there are changes that need to be made and how you can do your part to create the right environment.

_____

_____

_____

_____

_____

_____

_____

_____

Action: This chapter lists numerous practical ways to encourage your pastor. Now that you have finished reading, plan a time to meet with your pastor. If you have caused disunity or discouragement, seek his forgiveness. Verbally commit to being on his team, to publicly support him and his family, and to volunteer at the church as you are able.

Chapter 6 Notes

102 · LeJoia I. VanHook

CONCLUSION

You Are Not Alone

Now we ask you, brothers, to respect those who work hard among you, who are over you in the Lord and who admonish you. Hold them in the highest regard in love because of their work.
—1 Thessalonians 5:12–13 (NIV)

I truly pray that this book will improve the lives of pastors, open the eyes of the Church, and encourage congregations to readjust their expectations of church leaders.

Every church should strive to protect and support their pastor. No pastor deserves to feel alone in the ministry. I pray that this book encourages pastors to seek assistance when they are feeling depressed and burned out.

To the pastors who have read this book:

Please seek counsel for your needs, because your life is valuable, and it matters!

People are advocating for you to be successful. It is okay to make mistakes, because we are all human beings. But do not give up on what God has called you to do. He loves you, and He will not allow you to fail if you trust Him and seek His will.

To the church members who have read this book: Remember to encourage your pastors and remind them they are not alone. Seek for ways you can be a blessing to your pastor and your church. And pray with me:

Dear Heavenly Father,

We come to You, giving You all the glory, honor, and praise. You have been so good to us. We know You to be a Way-Maker, a Protector, a Provider, a Miracle Worker, and so much more. God, we ask that You forgive us of our sins, iniquities, and transgressions.

We come to You on behalf of the pastors of Your Church. Give them the strength to proclaim Your Word boldly to the nations. Help them to seek counsel when feelings of uncertainty, depression, or even suicide come over them. Help them to know that they are precious to You.

In the mighty name of Jesus, we come against the enemy who is trying to attack our pastors. Cover them with Your blood and wrap Your arms around them, we pray. Bless their families, for they sacrifice so much for Your Church. Bless them with overflow and abundance.

I pray that You help this book to change the mindsets of our congregations. Help us to be more understanding and supportive of our pastors. Help us to develop the habit of praying and fasting for them. Help us to give more to them and to the Church.

God, You are so good, and we bless Your holy name. We ask these things in the mighty and matchless name of Jesus. Amen.

REFERENCES

Notes

1. Daft, Richard L. *The Leadership Experience* (4th ed.). Thomas/South-Western, 2008.

2. Kouzes, J. M., and B. Z. Posner. *The Leadership Challenge* (4th ed.). Jossey-Bass, 2007.

3. "Who Is John Calvin Maxwell?" *Culture's Ways.* https://culturesways.com/leader-one-knows-way-goes-way-shows-way-john-c-maxwell.

4. Vaughn, Andy. "9 Ways to Support Your Pastor: Our Pastors Need Help, Too." *Beliefnet: Inspire Your Everyday.* http://www.beliefnet.com/faiths/christianity/articles/9-ways-to-support-your-pastor.aspx?.

5. McKenna, R. B., and K. Eckard. "Evaluating Pastoral Effectiveness: To Measure or Not to Measure." *Pastoral Psychology* no. 58 (2009): 303-313.

6. Ellison, C. W., and W. S. Mattila. "The Needs of Evangelical Christian Leaders in the United States."

Journal of Psychology and Theology 11, no. 1 (1983): 28–35.

7. Spaite, D. *Time Bomb in the Church: Defusing Pastoral Burnout.* Beacon Hill, 1999.

8. Bailey, Sarah Pulliam. "Isaac Hunter Dead: Summit Church Pastor and Son of Obama Advisor Joel Hunter Dies in Apparent Suicide." *HuffPost.* January 23, 2014. https://www.huffingtonpost.com/2013/12/11/isaac-hunter-dead_n_4427371.html.

9. "Pastor Burnout Statistics." *PastorBurnout.com.* Daniel Sherman. http://www.pastorburnout.com/pastor-burnout-statistics.html.

10. "Pastor Burnout Statistics." *PastorBurnout.com.* Daniel Sherman.

11. Mills, Harry, Natalie Reiss, and Mark Dombeck. "The Long-Term Consequences of Negative Stress." *Journal of Mental Health* (2008): 6.

12. *Greenleaf* (Season 2). Oprah Winfrey Network, 2017.

13. Vaughn, Andy. "9 Ways to Support Your Pastor."

14. Vaughn, Andy. "9 Ways to Support Your Pastor."

APPENDIX

Pastor Responses

Participating Pastor Codes (by Pseudonym)

P1= Pastor Steven
P2= Pastor Dwight
P3= Pastor Paul
P4= Pastor Harris
P5= Pastor Smithson
P6= Pastor Trenton
P7= Pastor Wright
P8= Pastor Randall
P9= Pastor Lowe
P10= Pastor Summers
P11= Pastor Jake
P12= Pastor West
P13= Pastor Blake

Table 1

Stressors from Within and Without

Pastor	Source of Stress
P7	Pressure from without: "Everything that seems to take place in society, there's always a blame it seems to put first on the pulpit. Every time something takes place in society, it's the pastors and the church that is at blame."
P10	Pressure from within: "In church, we don't want to say nothing to nobody, because we don't want to offend people. We don't want to come off as too hard, too rough, and so our members feel no need to get right. There's no conviction anymore."
P1	Pressure from without—part-time staff members add work: "I have to kind of work their responsibilities around the time that they're able to work and serve."
P12	Pressure from without: Government seeking to dictate how the church operates.
P10	Pressure from without: "Social media is the biggest downfall of the modern Church."
P10	Pressure of change: "The headache of dealing with going from traditional to contemporary."
P13	Pressure of change: "You have to marry the old with the new."
P8	Pressure of change: Church's growing pains.
P3	Pressure of change: "We change our methodologies to meet the needs of a modern Christian without being trendy."
P4	Pressure: "Expose the congregation to different or creative ways to do ministry to inspire

	and revitalize them."
P7	Pressure: "You're supposed to *continue* to be inspired [to inspire them]."
P10	Physical stress: "One is the stress of preaching—most of us are not lecturing preachers. We hoot, we holler, we run, we scream, we celebrate Jesus, right? The strain on your heart, your blood pressure, everything, is just like working an eight-hour hard-labor job in a thirty-minute sermon."
P12	Pressure to perform: "[The struggle to] get people to understand that going to church, the church is not the building."
P11	Pressure to perform: "Learn the culture of the church, understand the different dynamics involved in the church, such as the personalities and demographics."
P8	Pressure: "You got to understand culture—and each church has its own culture."

Table 2

Congregation-Related Stressors

Pastor	Source of Stress
P7	Shirking responsibility: "It's as if they want us to take over their homes, you know."
P6	"Am I doing all I can do? It becomes very stressful."
P10	"And God forbid that Deacon Jones says something that Sister Smith didn't like. Now you've got to deal with that conflict as well. You've got folks want to cuss each other out, you got folks want to fight one another because 'I didn't like the way she looked at me in the choir....'"
P12	"Church is not taken as seriously as it once was."
P9	"Falling away from worship [as] a gathering of people. ... Everyone feels as if they can connect to God and tune in to God on their own, and so there's no need for coming together with other believers."
P7	"Inside of the Church, especially in recent years, there have been a lot of different things that people want to bring into the Church that don't necessarily coincide with the doctrine of the Church or the accurate teachings of our particular local body."
P7	"People who have been part of the Church for a while—they're not very open to the new ideas or the new believers. ... So there's times when the pastor has to step in."
P7	"They had a hard time [with new things] be-

	cause they've been kind of institutionalized with a certain way that things were supposed to go. [They were not receptive to] the particular mindset [of] change [or how] the church is growing."
P7	"The pastor must deal with people with very different life experiences and expectations."
P6	"The people are not listening and they're not doing what they need to be doing to obtain the fullness of life. You become discouraged."
P4	"Resistance [of] the congregation to grow up [as they are] more comfortable in a position of mediocrity."
P12	"A lack of commitment from the [flock]."
P13	"Getting people to commit—it's a huge one."
P7	"They're not allowing the Spirit to continue to inspire them. They're locked into an old mindset, and they don't even know that they've been institutionalized. So, it's a constant battle."
P4	"Unrealistic expectations from the congregation, for example, expecting the pastor to be everywhere at the same time."
P10	"The other factor is the stress of people, so you've been dealing with [people] all week long with little stuff—but then on Sunday, all the people that didn't call you, didn't have your number, didn't have your e-mail, didn't bother you all week, you get *bombarded* with loads of foolishness on Sunday."
P6	"You have to see to the welfare of the people in general. People have all types of problems. We have to be able to discern them sometimes. Sometimes the people won't tell you right out."

| P8 | "You have to teach. There's some that's going to be receptive, and there's some that's not going to be." |

Table 3

Family-Related Stressors

Pastor	Source of Stress
P1	"Living in a fishbowl, for the family—it's a big one."
P6	"It affected my personal life tremendously. My wife, my children—they didn't understand the sacrifices that had to be made."
P1	"We give everything to the church, and there's not enough for wife, husband, children."
P4	"My family has been drafted into pastoring involuntarily and against my will. [Congregants] make demands on my family that are offensive to me, because my family does not pastor this church. I pastor this church, but they put them in awkward quagmires and very awkward situations that I don't think is fair."
P10	"You should start talking to the preachers' wives. And if they're honest, they will tell you how much it hinders your life. We preachers are called to be preachers and pastors, and so [we put] restrictions on ourselves. We then put on our families, but they're not the ones that are called to preach or pastor. [We do it] to keep our reputation together. We put that stress on our families, and it causes a strain. It does—it causes a real strain within family situations. It does."
P10	"And then on top of it, baby, you've left a contentious environment at the church [and] had an emergency trustee meeting because the

	roof of the church fell in. [When you get home] your wife is mad you stayed at the church two hours too long [and] your children are disappointed, they're mad. *The stress of all that, baby, will kill you. It can kill you.*"
P1	"We raise children who hate God, or they hate the God we showed them—the God that took Daddy from them, or the God that took Mom from them."

Table 4

Involvement-Related Stressors

Pastor	Source of Stress
P6	Pressure: "We don't receive the encouragement that we need."
P7	Pressure to perform: "Little do they know the pastor is doing quite a bit, [from] praying constantly for them to visiting the sick, coming to the prisons to visit their relatives and making calls and things like that—the pastor is always involved."
P10	Pressure to perform: "You no longer belong to yourself. In fact, there's very little time that you have for yourself, because there's always somebody pulling at you. The stuff that's thrown at you and the different directions you have to go in will *make the average person lose their mind.*"
P1	Messiah complex: "In the African American context, one of the dangers is the hero complex—the Savior complex. We put that pressure on ourselves where we have to do everything, so we're the first to get there and we're the last to leave."
P1	Pressure: "The Church just puts undue weight on people."
P2	Burnout: "A pastor becomes burnt out."
P1	Burnout: "I feel burnt out some days now."
P5	Pressure: "Most churches are the opposite [in that they drive the pastor to the point of collapsing]."
P5	Pressure: "Pastoring will always take you be-

| | yond the historical [logistics] that you're used to." |

Table 5

Stressors from the Loss of a Personal Life

Pastor	Source of Stress
P1	Loss of privacy: "Living in a fishbowl, for the family—it's a big one."
P10	Loss of outlets: "Because most ministers are men, we are programmed to hold everything in. By the time it comes out—or even if it doesn't come out, by the time we start dealing with it—it's so far gone that, you know, you almost can't help but.... It's just too far gone. It's too far gone."
P12	Loss of outlets: Carnality.
P10	Loss of personal life (isolating): "I don't hang out with my members. [They are too judgmental.]"
P10	Loss of personal life (isolating): "Paul said we are *prisoners for Christ*, and in a way we are. It can feel like a prison because there are places you can't go and things you can't do and people you can't be around. You never quite fit in a niche."
P4	Loneliness: "I think there's a great deal of loneliness in leadership."
P3	Loss of personal life and ideals: "Losing who you are because you're a spiritual leader ... will cause stress."
P7	Loss of personal life: "[Behavior outside the church] puts your reputation on the line, as well as the reputation of the Church as a whole."
P8	Loss of personal life: "[Being] a public suc-

	cess but a private failure. [The pastor] might be successful [at church], but you go home and your wife don't think [anything] of you. And your kids don't, either."
P1	Loss of personal life: "No or little life outside the church."
P13	Loss of personal life: "For the pastor himself individually, balancing church and personal [life] is a big challenge. It can be stressful, if you don't know how to balance it."
P12	Loss of personal life: "We cannot survive this by ourselves [without a solid circle of peers]."
P3	Loss of personal life: "One mistake pastors make is forming inappropriate alliances, because you have to be careful with the kind of people you let inside your life circle."
P4	Loss of personal life: "Pick your friends very wisely."
P7	Loss of personal life: "Separating yourself from what were previous relationships with people that were not conducive to growth."

Table 6

Stressors from Lack of Outlets and Pressures to Perform

Pastor	Source of Stress
P4	"Be prepared. There are a lot of blessings in pastoring, but it also comes with a lot of burdens, a lot of letdowns."
P10	"[The pastor must be] long-suffering."
P1	"Sometimes the realism can set in so strongly and so sternly that people lose their ability to dream."
P1	"You don't have time to do strategy because you're too busy playing firefighter. There's so much to do today that you don't have time to even look toward the future, so vision suffers and strategy suffers. You start doing day-to-day stuff."
P1	"If we don't get outlets, we major in what I call 'the dark arts'."
P10	"Honestly, there's a great deal of alcoholism within ministry because the stress level is just ridiculous."
P11	"It's incredibly important to know that there's a lot of pastors who are hurting, a lot of personal issues and things. Because we all can get the private demons sometimes to manifest and [get] attacked more than anybody else. ... *Unfortunately, pastors don't have a place to go to really be transparent and get help.*"
P2	"People will drive you to drink, drugs, or whatever—or to your vices—to the point you're not thinking."

Table 7

Pastoral Coping Mechanisms

Coping Mechanism	P1	P2	P3	P4	P5	P6	P7	P9	P10	P11	P12	P13
Avoiding social media									x			
Avoiding worry			x	x								
Board games		x										
Church					x							
Creativity at work				x								
Date night	x						x					
Doing what makes me happy			x									
Exercise, athleticism	x		x	x	x		x			x		
Faith		x	x						x		x	
Family time	x	x					x					
Fear of disappointing God	x											x
Keeping									x			

private life private													
Keeping the Sabbath	x												
Life outside the church	x												x
Modeling on Jesus		x			x								
Movies		x		x									
Multidimensional foresight				x									
Music		x		x	x								
Never giving up on goals									x		x	x	x
Novelty			x										
Pamper days										x			
Patience			x			x	x						
Planning			x							x			
Prayer	x	x			x	x	x	x	x		x		
Realistic acceptance				x									x
Retail therapy										x			
Self-knowledge	x												
Social	x	x	x	x		x	x	x			x		

support												
Step away			X			X	X	X		X		X
Stress-relieving state-ments					X							
Timing			X									
Vaca-tions	X		X			X			X			

About the Author

Dr. LeJoia VanHook graduated Magna Cum Laude with a Bachelor of Arts in Psychology and Spanish in 2010 from Fisk University. From there, she attended and graduated from Roosevelt University, where she received her Master of Arts degree in Training and Development in 2012. Upon graduating with her master's, Dr. VanHook immediately went on to pursue a doctorate in Organizational Leadership at Argosy University. She dedicated her dissertation to studying pastoral leadership and their experience with stress and burnout. When she chose her dissertation topic, she believed it was God calling her to be an ambassador for topics rarely addressed in the church.

LeJoia is an educator with an adaptable and accurate prophetic mantle over her life. She is not a pastor, yet she was led by the spirit to pen this dynamic guide to pastors. LeJoia shares a fiery message of deliverance, power, and purpose. Her passion for God and a surrendered lifestyle have led to an anointing to adhere to God's voice and direct His chosen. Her insightful message includes sobering truths that challenge men and women of God to pray and cultivate their God-given potential in their personal and spiritual lifestyles—and to prevent pastoral burnout.

LeJoia has a deep passion for needy and hurting people, out of which grew the mission for outreach that birthed this book. She is now the author of this guide, which is designed to enhance pastors by delivering quality resources, spiritual and psychological, which will improve the daily lives of pastors and their families. With humility and generosity of spirit, LeJoia captivates the minds and hearts of God's people and helps them lead productive lives.

LeJoia possesses the ability to reach people of all ages and various walks of life. Through her ministry, she strives to positively influence the lives of God's people through the application of the Word. Her hope is to inspire believers to walk upright and holy lives into higher dimensions.

No more burnout!

About Speak It To Book

Speak It to Book is revolutionizing how books are created and used.

Traditional publishing requires thousands of hours, and then you're asked to surrender your rights. Self-publishing is indicative of a poor-quality product with no prestige. And neither model boasts results-driven marketing.

That's why we created a better option. Speak It To Book has the attention of the industry because we are disrupting it in a brilliant way.

Imagine:

- What if you had a way to get those ideas out of your head?
- What if you could get your story in front of the people who need it most?
- What if you took the next step into significance and influence?

You can accomplish all of these goals by writing a book. Plus, you can do it without having to use a pencil, and in less than one-tenth of the time!

Your ideas are meant for a wider audience. So step into significance—by speaking your story into a book.

Visit www.speakittobook.com to learn more.

Made in the USA
Columbia, SC
04 June 2018